Date Due

JA-05 '0			
FEB 17			
JUL 16 '0			
AUG 08			
MAY 23			
JU 14			
MAR 17 0			

FEMALE SPORTS
STARS

CHELSEA HOUSE PUBLISHERS

FEMALE SPORTS
STARS

SUPERSTARS OF WOMEN'S FIGURE SKATING

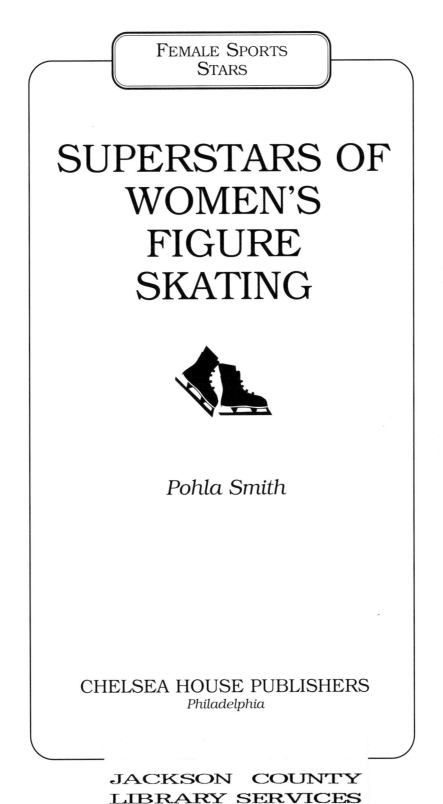

Pohla Smith

CHELSEA HOUSE PUBLISHERS
Philadelphia

CHELSEA HOUSE PUBLISHERS

Produced by Daniel Bial Agency and Associates
New York, New York

Senior Designer   Cambraia Magalhães
Picture Research   Sandy Jones
Cover Illustration   Bonnie Gardner
Frontispiece photo   Katarina Witt

3 5 7 9 8 6 4 2

Library of Congress Cataloguing-in-Publication Data

Smith, Pohla
      Superstars of women's figure skating / Pohla Smith.
        p.   cm.—(Female sports stars)
      Includes bibiliographical references and index.
      ISBN 0-7910-4392-4 (Hard)
        1. Women skaters—Biography—Juvenile literature. 2. Skating
—Juvenile literature. [1. Ice skaters. 2. Women—Biography.]
I. Title. II. Series.
GV850.A2S55   1997
796.91'2'0922—dc20
[B]   96-45755
                                                                                              CIP
                                                                                              AC

Contents

SONJA HENIE

Ice skating developed as a means of winter transportation at least a thousand years ago. Skating is believed to have been born in Scandinavia—the cold weather nations of Norway, Sweden, Finland, and Denmark.

The earliest skates were blades carved out of the bones of big animals like reindeer and laced onto shoes. They were a good way to get around during the long, cold winters when snow and ice covered every lake, stream and creek—even much of the land.

Racing on ice became more fun after iron was developed and forged into skating blades. They were very heavy and wore down quickly, but they were better than bones.

Skating began to grow and evolve more quickly into the sports of hockey, speed skat-

Sonja Henie performed at her first Olympics in 1924 at age 12. Here she takes time off to skate with Gillis Grafström, a seven-time world champion.

ing, and figure skating when lighter, more durable steel blades were invented by E. W. Bushnell in Philadelphia in 1850.

Figure skating dates back to at least 1772, when a Captain Robert Jones wrote what is credited as the first book on the subject in Great Britain. But back then, the sport was slow, stiff stroking. The emphasis was on perfect posture and straight arms and legs. Figure skaters looked more like goose-stepping soldiers than athletes.

In America, skating clubs concentrated on using the inside and outside edges of their blades to scratch fancy designs on the ice. They skated on one foot at a time. Those exercises developed into the compulsory, or school, figures that were a part of world and Olympic competitions until they were eliminated in 1991.

Meanwhile, an American man born around 1840 was getting ready to add an artistic element. Jackson Haines has been described as a ballet teacher, ballroom dancer, and an actor. Whatever his role in show business, he began skating to music, using ballet steps and moves to make skating prettier to watch. He called it the international style of skating.

Americans didn't take all that well to his style, but when Haines took his exhibitions to Europe they were very popular. Composers even began composing waltzes especially for skating. Haines' Vienna School of Skating produced a couple international champions, and the style spread to England. However, it still wasn't widely accepted in the United States.

Ice skating became popular enough around the world, though, that it was included in the Summer Olympics of 1908. Sixteen years later, Olympic officials decided to hold separate

Winter and Summer Games, and skating became a centerpiece of the cold weather festival. At those 1924 Winter Games, a young girl who would make history made her debut.

The world's first woman sports legend was just a little girl when she made her first international sports headlines. Her name was Sonja Henie (SOHN-ya HEN-ny), and she was a figure skater from Norway. She was only 11 years old when she traveled to Chamonix, France to represent her country in the 1924 Olympic Winter Games.

Sonja finished last among eight skaters. But she got a lot of attention anyway—partly because she was so young but primarily because of the way she skated.

During her routine, Sonja tried a jump. That was something females just weren't supposed to do back in those days. In fact, an American skater named Theresa Weld had been scolded by the male judges when she tried a jump in an earlier competition. Female skaters were supposed to look and move like dignified young ladies. In fact, most of Sonja's competitors wore long black dresses that would have made it hard to jump anyway. Sonja was allowed to skate in a shorter skirt because she was still a child, and she used the outfit to her advantage.

Sonja's free skating was much more athletic and stylish than the other skaters. And people loved the personality the little curly-haired blonde showed smiling at the crowd as she spun and twirled across the ice.

Three years later, at age 14, Sonja won her first world championship. At 15, she won the Olympic gold medal in the 1928 Winter Games at St. Moritz, Switzerland.

Once she got to the top of the amateur sports world, Sonja stayed there a long time—10 years. She went on to win a total of 10 world championships and three Olympic gold medals before retiring from amateur sports after the 1936 Olympics and world meets.

From the time she learned to skate at age 6 until she turned professional at age 24, Sonja won a total of 1,473 trophies, medals, and cups. In doing so, she changed the face of female figure skating from its prim and proper style to one more artistic, athletic, and dramatic.

For example, she introduced the first elements of choreography so important to skating today while winning her first Olympic medal in 1928. Choreography is the formal planning of dance, figure skating, and gymnastics routines to music. Sonja showed how to use dance steps and dramatic moves to link athletic skills like spins and jumps into one program that fits the music.

She also introduced some glamour to figure skating competition. Instead of plain dark dresses, she liked to wear white costumes trimmed with fur and white skates. She looked like a fairy tale princess.

Once Sonja turned professional, she moved to the United States, where she had the same huge impact on skating shows and the movies that she had had on amateur skating. She and her father persuaded a big Hollywood company to make a skating movie. She ended up signing a five-year contract with 20th Century Fox that was reported to have paid her $150,000 per movie. America was going through the Great Depression in the 1930s and that was a huge amount of money at that time—many people were lucky to make $1,500 a year. In fact,

Sonja's pay was more than many established movie stars were making. But she proved to be worth it.

Her movies were very glamorous and spectacular with lots of skaters, costumes, scenery, and special effects like black ice. Sonja also turned her traveling skating exhibitions into equally flashy spectaculars that set the style for popular shows today.

Movie fans started going to her ice shows, and skating fans went to her movies—over and over and over again. The sight of her skating so easily and glamorously gave them relief from the difficulties of their own lives.

Americans were crazy about this pretty, daring lady. They stormed airports when she flew into town, and sometimes police had to be called out to control crowds that gathered at her public appearances. Skating shows were sold out and thousands of little girls were inspired to try figure skating, a sport once thought to be only for the wealthy and high society.

But society loved her, too, and she became the first truly international female sports superstar, a name and face as well known as that of presidents, dictators, and movie idols. In fact, presidents and movie stars became her friends.

The movie company and the ice shows made Sonja lots of money. Sonja seemed to have the same business skills as her father, a

Henie shows off her graceful style while training for the 1936 Olympics.

world champion bicyclist who later became wealthy manufacturing fur coats. By the time Sonja died of cancer in 1969, she was reported to be worth 47 million dollars.

And skating had become big business. Ice rinks were built all over the United States to handle little girls who wanted to learn to skate like Sonja. More and more ice shows were developed to tour every part of the world.

Sonja has been a greater role model for American skaters than for her fellow Norwegians. Norway has not had an Olympic champion since Sonja in 1932. In fact, the best Olympic finish by a Norwegian since then is 22nd. But the United States has had five female gold medalists since Henie, along with a number of silver and bronze medalists. All of them can trace their style directly to the Norwegian skater-turned-movie star.

"Sonja was the pioneer. She was daring in the sport she loved," Tenley Albright once said. Tenley became the United States' first female Olympic skating champion at the 1956 Winter Games in Cortina, Italy.

"There is no other Sonja Henie. She made skating, especially women's skating," Carol Heiss said. Heiss, the American who succeeded Albright as Olympic champ in 1960, now is a successful coach.

But Tenley Albright, Carol Heiss, and the many great skaters who have followed in Sonja's footsteps have added to skating's appeal with grand stories of their own.

For example, Tenley overcame a non-paralyzing form of polio as a

Sonja Henie's movies were very popular and always featured several scenes of her skating.

little girl to become the U.S. skating champion. But two weeks before the Olympics she had a horrible mishap when she hit a rut in ice. Her left blade hit her right ankle and cut it to the bone. Tenley's father was a surgeon and stitched her up. Sore but determined, she was voted best by 10 of the 11 Olympic judges.

After the Olympics, Tenley went to Harvard Medical School and, like her father, she became a surgeon.

Carol Heiss's story also is dramatic. Her mother was suffering from cancer but went along with her daughter to the Cortina Olympics. She got to see Carol finish second, and a few weeks later Carol upset Tenley to win the world championship. Her mother never got to see her win the 1960 Olympic gold medal, though, for she died in October 1956.

Equally moving stories have been written by many of the world's skating queens. Jill Trenary, for example, came back from an even more serious skating injury to become a world champion. Another world champion, Japan's Midori Ito, had to leave home and move in with her coach at age 6 in order to keep training after her parents divorced. Oksana Baiul, the 1994 Olympic champion, overcame the desertion of her father, the deaths of her mother and grandparents, and the defection of her coach from the Soviet Union.

Does skating bring out the best in these young women? Or is it their determination to find success and happiness that makes them so successful?

You can try to decide for yourself as you read the inspiring stories of some of the female skating legends that follow.

PEGGY FLEMING

One of the things people noticed about defending world champion Peggy Fleming when the 1967 world championships got underway in Vienna, Austria, was that she had no bruises on her legs. The top skaters usually have at least one bruise somewhere on their legs or hips—and most of those bruises usually are pretty big and ugly.

All skaters—even the best ones—fall. And if the top skaters fall while they are practicing their jumps or spins, it really hurts. That's because they are skating so fast and jumping so high they crash harder than people who just skate around for fun.

But Peggy's legs were bruise-free as the world's best female skaters began tracing the school figures that were such a big part of competition back then.

By 1968, Peggy Fleming had won the U.S. national title five times and the world championship twice. But she only became a huge star after she won the Olympics that year.

The slender 18-year-old with the pretty dark hair and cute freckles just didn't fall very often—not even doing her double Axel jump. Though females skating today perform triple Axels, in 1967 the double Axel was the hardest jump any girl or woman was trying. In a double Axel, the skater takes off on one leg, does two-and-a-half-spins in the air, and comes down on the other leg.

By that year, Peggy was a three-time U.S. champion. One of her most famous moves was a spread eagle—or open-legged glide—into a double Axel into another spread eagle. It takes a lot of strength and athletic ability and body control to do a move like that, but Peggy made it look easy.

She always made skating look easy. And in some ways it was. Peggy was a natural on skates from the start. Unlike most beginners, Peggy didn't fall when she first tried ice skating. Her older sister, Janice, told reporters, "She didn't wobble or anything, she just started skating as though she had been at it for a long time."

Though skating came more naturally to her than it did to other people, Peggy had to overcome many barriers. For one thing, her parents moved their family of four daughters around a lot when Peggy was first starting to skate, and she had to change coaches several times.

In 1961, when Peggy was 12 and starting to really improve under a new coach she really liked, he was killed in an airplane crash. William Kipp, one of the nation's top coaches, was traveling with the U.S. team to the world championships championships in Prague, Czechoslovakia, when the plane crashed in Belgium. The entire team of skaters and all their coaches were killed.

Another problem was the fact that figure skating is expensive, and the Flemings didn't have a lot of money. Peggy's father, Albert, was a printer for newspapers, and he also took a part-time job to help pay for Peggy's lessons and ice time. He even learned to clean and make ice with a Zamboni machine.

Peggy's mother, Doris, sewed all of Peggy's skating dresses—even the ones she wore in the Olympics.

When Peggy finally was ready to go compete in her first nationals, she worried she wouldn't look as good as the other girls because she couldn't afford fancy store-made dresses and beauty shop hairdos. But her coach, Doriann

Judges watch carefully as Peggy Fleming completes her compulsory figures at the 1968 Olympics. In those days, marks from the compulsory-figure session counted as 50 percent of the final score.

Swett told the 13-year-girl it didn't matter, that she already had "the best equipment money can't buy."

"What's that?" Peggy asked.

"You and your own two legs," Miss Swett answered. "Lots of kids would love to skate as well as you do, Peggy. They don't have the talent, so they surround themselves with frills and feathers to hide what's missing in their performance."

In 1964, Peggy won her first U.S. title. She went to the Olympics, where she finished sixth, and then on to the worlds, where she came in seventh. While touring Europe with the world's top skaters that spring, Peggy and her mother learned Peggy's father had had a serious heart attack.

Peggy believed it would be too tough for the family to keep paying for her lessons while her dad got better. She said she was going to quit skating. But her parents and sisters Janice, Maureen, and Cathy wouldn't let her.

Her sisters already were sacrificing a lot. Because their mother had to spend so much time sewing costumes, driving Peggy to practice, or traveling to competitions and exhibitions, they took over a lot of the household chores. Janice did the cooking, for example, and Maureen mowed the lawn. The girls also made many of their own clothes.

So Peggy kept skating and won a second national title in Lake Placid, New York, in 1965. She also finished third in the world championships, which were held in Colorado Springs, Colorado. Peggy was happy to get third, because she had tired in the high altitude of the Rocky Mountains. The Flemings' home in Pasadena, California, had a low altitude, and it was hard for Peggy to get used to the thin Colorado air.

In 1965, the Flemings agreed to make still another sacrifice to help Peggy's skating. They moved to Colorado Springs. Peggy would train with world-famous coach Carlo Fassi. That way, she wouldn't get so tired when the 1966 worlds were held in the high altitude of Davos, Switzerland.

Peggy improved a lot working with Carlo— especially on her compulsory figures. She easily won her third straight U.S. championship.

In Davos, the time she had spent on improving her school figures paid off. After the compulsories, Peggy led defending champion Petra Burka of Canada by 49 points going into the free skating, at which many people already believed Peggy to be the best. But Peggy knew a win would not be easy. After all, only four people had ever defeated a reigning champion in the history of figure skating.

Peggy proved she was a champion the next night, though, skating the entire four-minute program without any major errors. When the competition was over, Peggy got the first-place ordinals of all nine judges. She won the title by 63 points over Gabrielle Seyfert of East Germany. Petra Burka came in third.

After the worlds, the top skaters went on tour again. But halfway through it, Peggy flew home to do a special skating exhibition in Boston. Her dad surprised her by driving all the way from Colorado to meet her there.

Just after Peggy got back to Europe for the rest of the tour, she heard the dreadful news that her father had had another heart attack and died while traveling back to Colorado. After the funeral, Peggy once again told her mother and sisters she planned to quit skating. She was afraid there wouldn't be enough money for her to train through the Olympics. She said she felt they had sacrificed enough.

But they wouldn't let her quit.

"I want Peggy to win a gold medal at the Olympics," Maureen said during a family conference.

"I won't let them down," Peggy promised.

And she didn't. In 1967, she won her fourth U.S. title. Then she flew to Vienna, Austria, where she won her second world championship even though she fell on a double Axel. After sliding across the ice, Peggy got up and skated her program so well that the crowd gave her a standing ovation. She ended up beating Seyfert this time by 94 points.

Peggy Fleming shows off her style during a practice in Grenoble in 1968.

Peggy graduated from high school that spring and began college in the fall, but she concentrated mostly on skating. She got two perfect scores of 6.0 in to win her fifth U.S. championship. Soon after, she was on her way to Grenoble, France, where NBC was going to televise the Winter Games live and in color for the first time.

After the two days of compulsory figures, Peggy had what seemed like an unbeatable lead—77 points over Seifert.

A reporter asked if she was going to "play it safe" in the free skating.

The question made Peggy angry. "What kind of champion would I be then?" she demanded. "My dad taught me to always do my best. Tomorrow night, I'm going to give it all I've got."

Her double Axel could have been stronger, but everything else went well. She burst into tears when she got off the ice and hugged her mother and Coach Fassi. Millions of Americans had just seen her win the gold medal.

After the Olympics, Peggy won another world title and then retired from amateur skating to turn professional. Money would never be a problem again. She signed a TV contract reported to be worth half-a-million dollars to do six TV specials. She signed contracts for commercials, and she signed a four-year contract to skate with the Ice Follies.

Peggy was America's sweetheart. There were parades and ceremonies in her honor. President Lyndon B. Johnson even invited her to eat lunch at the White House in 1968, twice! Little girls begged their mothers for skating lessons so they could be another Peggy Fleming.

Today, she is still looked upon as the brightest of all of America's figure skating stars.

DOROTHY HAMILL

Little girls and grown-up women raced to beauty salons after the 1976 Olympic Winter Games in Innsbruck, Austria. They wanted to get their hair cut in a "wedge" like figure skater Dorothy Hamill had when she won the gold medal.

It was a short haircut, and when she would spin, the cut made her thick brown hair fan around her like a brown halo. When she stood still, her hair showed off her pretty, heart-shaped face.

Twenty years later, the haircut is still popular. And so is Dorothy Hamill.

Like Sonja Henie and Peggy Fleming before her, she became a big celebrity after the Olympics. And, like Sonja and Peggy, she enjoyed a long and successful career as a professional skater and television celebrity.

Dorothy Hamill became a huge star after she won a gold medal at the Olympics in 1976.

She was inducted into the U.S. Figure Skating Hall of Fame in 1991, but she kept skating through the mid-1990s. That was nearly 30 years to the day after she got her first skates!

Dorothy looked much the same in 1996 as she did when she won the Olympic gold by sweeping the first-place votes of all nine judges in the free-skating finals. She said she felt she actually had become a more artistic skater with age.

The day Dorothy won the Olympic gold medal, she wore a red skating dress trimmed with white. As she stood on the bright ice, clutching some of the many bouquets of flowers thrown at her, some people thought she looked like a fairy-tale queen. Others were reminded of another Dorothy—the one who traveled down the Yellow Brick Road with Toto, the Scarecrow, the Tin Man, and the Cowardly Lion to find the Wizard of Oz.

Both comparisons were good ones, for Dorothy Hamill's long journey to Innsbruck reads much like a bedtime story.

Sure, Dorothy had some scares and excitement on the way, like the leg injury that interfered with training for the 1975 competition season. And she had to work very hard and give up the social life other teenagers enjoyed. But mostly, she had a lot of fun and success doing what she liked doing more than anything else.

Dorothy's "Yellow Brick Road" to the Olympics started at a little pond near her home in Riverside, Connecticut. Dorothy was 8 1/2 years old, and she had received a pair of ice skates as a Christmas gift. She liked skating right away. But she wasn't great at it from the start. She wanted to learn to skate backwards and spin around like some of the other skaters on the pond.

When she went home that day, Dorothy asked her mother if she could take lessons. In January, she joined a class that had started in November. By the time the class ended in March, Dorothy was the best skater.

She took more lessons that summer, and a teacher realized Dorothy had the ability to be very good. She asked Dorothy if she would like to learn the things she needed to know to compete. Of course, she said.

Dorothy started studying the school figures the U.S. Figure Skating Association requires competitors to learn. Then she took the first of eight tests all the skaters took as they moved up through the ranks of competition.

In December 1965, a year after she got her first skates, Dorothy passed her first test. Her career as a competitor was on its way.

The freckle-faced little girl was a fast learner. By December 1966, Dorothy had passed the second test, too. And she participated in her first competition, at the Juvenile Ladies' Level. From there, the skaters move to Novice, then Intermediate, and then Juniors. The last level of competition is Seniors. All Olympics are Senior-level champions.

Dorothy made a really big and important move when she was 12. She moved to New York City to stay with friends of her family so she could take lessons from 1951 U.S. champion Sonya Klopfer Dunfield. Dorothy enrolled in a new school and began skating with Sonya three hours a day.

That winter, Dorothy qualified for her first national competition, the 1969 novice championships in Seattle, Washington. She flew there with Sonya and skated so well, the judges named Dorothy novice champion of the United States. And she still was just 12!

Dorothy hit her first bump in the "Yellow Brick Road" soon after. She had moved up to junior competition and was hoping to qualify for the nationals at that level. But she fell over a rope on the ice and hurt her head during a practice session at the regional qualifiers in Buffalo, New York. Her doctor wouldn't let her finish the competition.

Dorothy made it to the 1970 junior nationals and she finished second at age 13 1/2. It was at those nationals in Tulsa, Oklahoma, that Dorothy first became known for the Hamill Camel. At the time, the spin didn't have a name. It simply was a new move that one of her coaches, Gustave Lussi, had invented for her. Dorothy then perfected it.

The move began with a regular layover camel, a jump in which the skater jumps with one leg extending backwards in the air while the skater is bent at the waist. The skater lands on the other leg with the push off the leg extended and spins. After that, Dorothy would bend her skating leg and drop into a sit spin.

After the junior nationals someone asked what she called it. She said it was just a variation of a camel. No one knows who actually came up with the clever name "Hamill Camel." But as soon as newspaper reporters started using it, it stuck. What an honor! There were only a few moves named for skaters, like the Axel, Lutz, and the Salchow jumps, and those skaters had been older and more famous when the moves were named.

But Dorothy was starting to get famous, too—at least in figure skating. She moved up to seniors in 1971, and even though she was only 14, she finished fifth. Skating officials were so impressed they asked her to go to a special event in Sapporo, Japan. That was where the Olympics would be held in 1972. Dorothy finished third at that event, her first international competition. Later that year, she won two other international competitions, the International Grand Prix in France and the Nebelhorn Trophy in West Germany.

It was while she was in Japan that she met Carlo Fassi, Peggy Fleming's old coach. She decided to study with him that summer. Dorothy's goal was to improve enough to make the United States' 1972 Olympic team.

Almost, but not quite. Dorothy was fourth at the 1972 U.S. nationals. Only the top three skaters made the team for the Olympics in Sapporo, Japan, where American Janet Lynn won the silver medal behind Beatrix Schuba of Austria.

But right after the Olympics, one of the other U.S. team members retired from amateur skating. Dorothy got to take her place at the 1972 world championships, and she finished seventh.

That summer, Dorothy moved to Denver, Colorado, to train full-time with Carlo Fassi. It

After her amateur career was over, Hamill made a lot of money skating for the Ice Capades and on prime-time television shows.

was tough for Dorothy to change schools and leave friends and family behind.

"But if I want to be a skater, that's the way it's got to be," Dorothy said in an interview with a reporter. "My coach lives in Denver, and I've got to be there too."

The move paid off. In 1973, Dorothy moved up to Number 2 at U.S. nationals behind Janet Lynn, and she finished fourth at the world championships.

When Janet Lynn announced she was turning professional, Dorothy set her sights on winning the 1974 U.S. title. And so she did that February, before a sold-out arena in Providence, Rhode Island. Her long program was so good, the fans pounded on the metal rails and seats.

Then it was on to worlds in Munich, West Germany, where Dorothy won the silver medal.

Following high school graduation that summer, Dorothy began putting even more time into her skating. She was getting better and better in this last year before the Olympics. Then, she hurt her foot while practicing, and she had to have it in a cast for a couple months. By the time it came off, it was only a month before nationals. She got in shape quickly enough to win her second straight U.S. title anyway, and then again finished second at the worlds, behind Dianne deLeeuw of the Netherlands. People couldn't help but wonder if Dorothy could have won without the lost training time.

The rest of 1975 went quickly, as the countdown to 1976 and the Innsbruck Winter Games started. Before she knew it, Dorothy had her third straight U.S. title and was on her way to Austria. All of her family—her mother, father, sister, brother, and sister-in-law—went, too.

Dorothy vowed to do her very best, and, sure enough, she did very well in the opening round of compulsory school figures. She finished second — in great shape to win the gold medal. Then she won the short program event that had been added to the competition to move into the lead.

Onto the finals. Dorothy skated to music from a movie called *The Seahawk*. And that's exactly how she skated—soaring into the air with strength and gliding across the ice with grace. The judges awarded her nearly all 5.8s and 5.9s, and she won the Olympic title. Afterward, she went on to the worlds and won it, too.

Like Peggy Fleming, Dorothy was a huge celebrity. After the usual world and Olympic tours, Dorothy joined the Ice Capades as a principal skater. She also went on to be the star of four prime-time television specials for ABC.

But Dorothy's adult years have not been all happiness. She and her first husband, Dean Paul Martin, were divorced, and he was later killed in a plane crash. She remarried, but in the fall of 1995, Dorothy and Ken Forsythe announced they were separating. When the Ice Capades got in trouble in 1993, Dorothy bought it. But the company continued to struggle, and Dorothy sold it.

Still Dorothy remains a beloved person in sports and among children. She does a lot of work for charities, like Big Brothers/Big Sisters and Special Olympics. She also teaches blind children how to skate. For Dorothy knows it is always good to have friends helping you as you travel down life's "Yellow Brick Road."

KATARINA WITT

Between 1983 and 1988, Katarina Witt won six European championships, four world titles, and two Olympic gold medals. No one had dominated amateur skating for that long since Sonja Henie.

Katarina skated for East Germany, a country that no longer exists. Her reign started when she upset defending world champion Rosalynn Sumners of the United States at the 1984 Olympics. It ended when she turned professional after the 1988 Olympics and world championships.

In between, she faced many, many talented, tough challengers: Americans Sumners, Tiffany Chin, Debi Thomas, and Jill Trenary; France's Surya Bonaly; Canada's Elizabeth Manley; Kira Ivanova of the old Soviet Union; and Midori Ito of Japan.

Americans generally did not root for athletes from Communist countries. But East Germany's Katarina Witt was so great everyone had to appreciate her. Here she skates for the gold at the 1984 Olympics.

But only one of them—Debi Thomas—ever beat Witt. And Debi did it just once, at the 1986 world championships.

Katarina had it all: solid jumps, great artistry, and a beautiful way of communicating with the audience, including the judges. Even her rivals sometimes found themselves cheering for her.

The only thing that Katarina could not beat was age. In 1993, when she was 28, she was reinstated as an amateur and made the 1994 German Olympic team. This time, however, she could not do as many of the triple jumps as younger skaters like Oksana Baiul, Nancy Kerrigan and Chen Lu. Nor did she skate a mistake-free long program. She finished seventh overall.

But Witt didn't let it get her down. She returned to the professional ranks and, now in her 30s, still delights fans with her beautiful skating and artistry. She says she plans to skate as long as she is able.

Katarina already has been skating more than a quarter of a century. She was only five when she took her first lessons.

It was lucky for Katarina that she and her parents and brother lived in the East German city of Karl-Marx-Stadt. In old communist countries like East Germany and the Soviet Union, the governments ran the top sports programs. Coaches recruited children who appeared to have the body type or athletic ability to do well in certain sports and sent them to live in national training centers.

Karl-Marx-Stadt was the site of a figure skating training center. Katarina passed the center walking home from school, and she would stop to watch the children skate on the outdoor rink. She begged her mother to join the skating club. But when her mother took Katarina to sign up for lessons, the teacher said it was too late for the current session. Katarina cried until the teacher let her in.

Because she was so good, the skating association sent Katarina to a new coach when she was 9. The coach was Jutta Muller, the best in East Germany and one of the top coaches in the world. Two years later, at age 11, Katarina landed her first triple jump. Coach Muller gave her a cash reward, 20 German marks, or about $7.50 in American currency.

Because her parents lived nearby, Katarina never did have to move into the Sport Club Karl-Marx-Stadt. But, though she lived at home, she spent more and more time with her coach. In between regular school, Katarina practiced for four or five hours a day. She also worked another hour daily on building strength.

In addition, Frau Muller taught Katarina how to be a performer. Katarina learned how to look at the audience and pull them into her performance. She learned how to put on makeup and interpret music.

Katarina earned her first major medal at 17, when she placed third in the 1983 European championships. By the next year, she was ready to take on the whole world.

Katarina Witt's main opponent was Debi Thomas of the U.S. With this performance, Thomas edged Witt to win the gold at the 1986 world championships.

She went to the 1984 Olympics in Sarajevo as the European champion, where Rosalynn Sumners, the defending world and two-time U.S. champion, was the favorite.

But the 17-year-old Katarina made quite a splash in her Olympic debut. After the first two of the three events in women's singles, she was first. Sumners was second, and Kira Ivanova was third.

Whoever among them won the long program finale would win the gold. Katarina was about to show for the first time that she was just as tough mentally as she was physically talented and beautiful.

Katarina skated to American music and landed three clean triple jumps. Her artistry was equally exciting, and her scores were mostly 5.8s and 5.9s. There was room for Rosalynn Sumners to win, but she would have to give her very best.

But Rosalynn got conservative near the end of her program. She turned one planned triple jump into a double and did a single rather than the planned double Axel.

Katarina got the gold, Rosalynn the silver, and Kira the bronze.

Katarina went on to win the 1984 world championships, too. Rosalynn turned professional, but Ivanova kept skating.

There were other young skaters coming up behind Katarina. The next year, 1985, American Tiffany Chin was being compared to Peggy Fleming and Dorothy Hamill.

It was when Tiffany and Katarina met at the 1985 worlds that Katarina really showed her mental toughness.

Usually, figure skaters do not watch each other's performances. It makes them too nervous. But after Witt skated her program, she came back out to the side of the rink to watch Tiffany. To some observers, it seemed that Katarina psyched out Tiffany, for Tiffany skated badly. She singled one triple and then fell on a double Axel. Katarina won her second straight world championship.

In 1986, Katarina began a new, long-lasting, and much more threatening rivalry. That was the year that Debi Thomas, a Stanford University student hoping to become a doctor, became the United States' first African-American skating champion.

Debi's style was much different than Katarina's. Debi was lean and athletic-looking —she even preferred to skate in a unitard, a leotard with built-in leggings. Katarina looked more like a movie star with flashy, glitzy costumes. Debi skated with great power—her style fit the hard rock music she liked to skate to. Katarina's style was more artistic. Katarina's life revolved around skating. Debi tried to juggle schoolbooks and skating.

Katarina went to the 1986 championships in Geneva, Switzerland, as the favorite. But she made what was for her a rare mistake skating her short program: She was not able to complete the required jump combination. That left her in fourth place going into the long program finale.

Like a true champion should, Katarina rose to the challenge. Many later called her program the best of her career. Her technical moves were difficult and well-done. Her presentation was even better. Two of the judges gave her perfect 6.0s for her artistry.

However, all Debi had to do to win the title was finish second in the long program.

*Debi Thomas and
Katarina Witt both skat-
ed as Carmen at the
1988 Olympics. Witt was
both sexier and brought
more emotion—and
became the first woman
to repeat as champion
since Sonja Henie.*

Katarina came out to watch, but Debi did not allow herself to get nervous. She landed four clean triple jumps and skated enthusiastically. The judges ruled her second-best that night, and Debi took the gold medal. Katarina settled for silver.

The next year, 1987, the world championships were to be held in the American city, Cincinnati, Ohio. The upcoming battle between Thomas and Witt got a lot of publicity. But this year it would be a three-way struggle: Debi had gone to nationals suffering from sore tendons, and a younger skater named Jill Trenary had upset her for the 1987 U.S. title.

Jill was an 18-year-old native of Minneapolis, Minnesota, who just two years earlier had suffered a career-threatening injury. Jill's calf muscles were cut through during an on-ice collision with another skater. She had to have surgery to sew them back together.

Who would skate best? More important, who would be toughest?

Jill and Katarina both got off to a bad start. Witt finished fifth in the compulsories, and Trenary finished sixth. Debi was second.

Katarina cried that day, but by the next day she was ready to fight again. She went out and won the short program competition. Debi slipped on her required double Axel and finished seventh.

They went into the finals with Katarina second behind Kira Ivanova, who was not as good a free skater as the others, and Debi third.

Debi skated before Katarina, and, despite her sore tendons, she did one of the best long programs of her life. She landed five triples and two double Axels.

Katarina was going to have to be great to win. And, she was. Skating with her usual artistry, she did three triple jumps and two double Axels. Katarina reclaimed the world title, and everyone in skating turned their sights to the Olympics. Would Debi and Katarina have another duel in the Winter Games in Calgary, Canada, in 1988?

Did they ever!

Katarina and Debi actually began a war of words months before the Olympics. Both women had decided to skate their Olympic long programs to music from the opera "Carmen." As one reporter put it, that was kind of like two rivals showing up at a party in the same dress.

Neither woman would change, though. Instead they made little insulting remarks about each other. It was the kind of psychological warfare that goes on in many big-time sports.

Finally, in February, the war moved to the ice. Debi took the first round, finishing ahead of Katarina in the compulsory figures event.

Then came the short program. Each woman did all the mandatory moves cleanly and skated well. But they skated very differently. Katarina actually tap-danced on ice to music from Broadway shows. Debi rocked in her unitard to a disco tune.

The judges liked Witt's program better and ranked Thomas second behind her. But after two rounds, Debi stood first overall and Witt was second.

Either could win the gold by beating the other in the long program finale. It was on to the final duel between the two Carmens.

Katarina competed several skaters before Debi. Katarina followed Japan's Midori Ito, who had wowed everyone by landing seven triple jumps. Compared to Midori, Katarina's routine seemed too easy. She landed four triples and left another planned triple out. The judges gave her good marks, but there was plenty of room for Debi to beat her.

As usual, Katarina came out to watch her rival. What she saw gave her confidence she would win.

On her first big move, a triple-jump combination, Debi two-footed the landing of the second jump. A look of panic moved across Debi's face. She never recovered her poise. She made mistakes on two more triple jumps. She scored so poorly that she ended up having to settle for the bronze medal. Katarina became the first skater to win back-to-back Olympic titles since Sonja Henie in 1936. Elizabeth Manley of Canada came from behind to pass Debi for the silver. Jill Trenary was fourth.

Then they went on to the worlds, where Katarina won again, while Debi was third. Then they both turned professional.

Katarina didn't have the same opportunities to make money as American skaters because the Communist government had to give permission for everything she did. But when the Communist government fell and East and West Germany were reunited in 1990, Katarina was free to travel.

Like all the skating queens before her, she has toured the United States with ice shows and made skating movies. She now considers both Berlin, Germany, and New York City home.

But as much as she enjoys life as a pro, she called her third trip to the Olympics as an aging amateur her most satisfying. It was the first time her parents were free to come see her skate, and there was no government telling her she had to win to stay in good graces. All she had to do was enjoy skating. And she did.

"I feel this is much more coming from inside me now," Witt said before the Olympics. "I couldn't have done this 10 years ago."

5

KRISTI YAMAGUCHI

At birth, Kristi Yamaguchi didn't look much like a future Olympic champion. Her legs were so crooked that doctors immediately put her feet in casts. After the casts came off, she had to wear clumsy corrective shoes.

As she got a little older, her mother, Carole, suggested she take dancing and ice skating lessons to make her legs stronger.

Kristi already had an interest in skating. At age 4 1/2, she had watched Dorothy Hamill win her Olympic gold medal on television. She had a Dorothy Hamill doll that she carried with her everywhere.

Then, when she was six, her mother took her to see an ice show. Kristi was hooked. "I kept asking my mom to take me every week, and I was competing by the time I was eight," Kristi said.

Kristi Yamaguchi twirls while holding her skate blade. This performance at the 1992 Olympics won her the gold medal.

Kristi became a wonderful skater. And her feet and legs grew straight and very strong—strong enough to carry her all the way to the 1992 Olympic Winter Games. Then, in Albertville, France, she did what no American woman had done since her heroine Dorothy Hamill in 1976: win the Olympic gold medal.

Even though she was the 1991 world champion, Kristi was stunned to win the Olympics. She was only 21. She had thought her best chance to win an Olympic title would come in 1994, at the Winter Games scheduled for Norway.

But her fans weren't all that surprised. They had gotten used to seeing Kristi do the unexpected. She had been doing just that since the 1989 U.S. championships, where she established herself as a fast-rising star and chief rival to Jill Trenary.

Debi Thomas had turned professional after the 1988 Olympics. Jill, who had finished fourth at the Calgary Winter Games, was favored to win the 1989 U.S. title.

And she did. But Kristi still managed to steal the show. A wonderful jumper, she skated a beautiful and exciting long program. The judges placed her first in that event.

Though Kristi had done poorly in compulsory figures, that showing in the long program was enough to give the 17-year-old from Fremont, California, the silver medal.

And that wasn't all. Kristi also won a gold medal in pairs with her 19-year-old partner Rudy Galindo that year. To do so, they upset 1988 Olympic veterans Natalie and Wayne Seybold.

Kristi was the first woman to medal in two U.S. national events since Margaret Graham in 1954—35 years earlier!

When Kristi was young, she competed in pairs competition with Rudy Galindo. In 1986, Galindo set a record by winning medals for both pairs and single competitions at the same world championship. Of course, Kristi won her share of medals for both types of competition as well!

The reason so few women had won in two events is because it is so difficult to skate and train in more than one. Kristi kept an amazing schedule.

For years, Kristi would get up at 4:00 in the morning and practice five hours on her singles. After school, Kristi would join Rudy for pairs practice. For two years, she even tried studying

Jill Trenary celebrates the terrific performance that won her the 1988 world championship.

at home rather than at school, but she missed the activity. She usually went to bed before 8 p.m.

Her pairs coach, Jim Hulick, told reporters at the 1989 nationals in Baltimore, Maryland, that Kristi was "superhuman." It seemed the perfect word for the tiny skater. In Baltimore, she was always bustling off to another practice session when other singles or pairs skaters were getting ready to rest or to go shopping.

After Baltimore, Kristi and Rudy went on to the 1989 world championships in Paris, France. Kristi finished sixth in singles behind champion Midori Ito of Japan, a great jumper who forced Jill Trenary to settle for second place. Rudy and Kristi were fifth in pairs.

Kristi's life became even busier and harder that year, when her singles coach, Christy Kjarsgaard, moved to Edmonton, Alberta, to get married. Kristi began commuting between her home in California, where she trained with Rudy and Coach Hulick, and Canada, where she trained with Christy.

Then, Coach Hulick died of AIDS-related cancer, and Kristi and Rudy had to find another pairs coach.

Officials with the United States Figure Skating Association were pressuring Kristi to give up one event. But Kristi stuck with both through the 1990 season.

She and Rudy won a second straight U.S. pairs title and again finished fifth at the 1990 world champions in Halifax, Canada. She also won her second straight silver medal behind Trenary at the 1990 nationals. But in singles at the worlds, Kristi moved up from her sixth-place finish in 1989 to fourth.

USFSA officials really believed Kristi could become a world and Olympic champion if she made a choice and concentrated on one event. They wanted it to be singles.

Finally, after the 1990 competition season ended, Kristi did choose to give up pairs. She moved to Edmonton, Canada, to train full-time with Christy Kjarsgaard, who now was called Christy Kjarsgaard Ness.

Though Kristi had skater-friends in Calgary, she was homesick.

"It was hard to be apart from my family that first year," Kristi said later. "I moved the day after high school graduation, so I missed the parties and that feeling of 'school's out.' I called home a lot—my sister Lori and my brother Brett and I are pretty close."

But the tough decision and the change in lifestyle soon would pay off.

In 1991, Jill Trenary suffered a major injury and needed surgery on her right ankle. She could not compete at the nationals or worlds. Meanwhile, a new rule took effect, eliminating compulsory figures from competition. Kristi wouldn't have to worry about bad school-figure scores pulling down her finish.

Kristi was the favorite to win the 1991 nationals at Minneapolis, Minnesota. But she got out-jumped by another skater named Tonya Harding, the first and only American woman to land a triple Axel. Kristi had her second straight silver medal.

Kristi worked very hard between nationals and worlds to perfect the Axel. But she just couldn't master it that fast. She knew that both Harding and Japan's Midori Ito of Japan probably would do triple Axels during the competition in Munich, Germany. Though her other triple jumps were very strong, and though Kristi was the most artistic of the three skaters, she wasn't sure that would be enough.

They were, though—thanks in part to a couple breaks that were lucky for her and unlucky for the competition.

When the skaters were warming up for the short program, Midori Ito collided with another skater and bruised her ribs. Then, while skating her routine, she landed a triple jump too close to the boards. She flew over the side of the rink. This error caused her to finish third in the short program. Kristi skated a clean short program and finished first.

Kristi still needed to finish first in the long program, or free skating, to win the gold, though. And that was where she was afraid not having a triple Axel would hurt her.

But all the top challengers made mistakes.

Ito was in pain with her bruised ribs and sore left ankle. She fell once and landed only four of her eight triples.

Surya Bonaly, another great jumper from France, fell twice.

Tonya Harding did her triple Axel, but she made a big mistake on a combination. Instead of a triple toe-triple toe, she did a single and a double.

Kristi didn't see any of the mistakes. She was skating last, and she just went out on the ice determined to do her best, which she did.

She was very athletic—she landed six triple jumps cleanly. And she was artistic: She got seven 5.9s and one perfect 6.0 for artistic impression!

Kristi won the gold medal, and the United States swept the competition. Harding took the silver, and Nancy Kerrigan, who would become very famous a couple years later, won the bronze medal.

Jill Trenary didn't recover from her ankle surgery in time to try to qualify for the 1992 Olympics at the U.S. Nationals, either. She sat out both competitions and then turned professional that spring.

Midori Ito of Japan acknowledges the crowd's applause as she prepares to accept her silver medal at the 1992 Olympics. Kristi Yamaguchi stands on the highest podium having already accepted the gold.

But no one expected Midori Ito to have the same kind of bad luck at the Olympics that she had had in 1991. If she skated and jumped her best, she would be impossible to beat.

Harding also would be tough if she hit all her jumps, and some people thought Surya Bonaly, another great jumper, might benefit from skating before a home crowd in France.

Some reporters wrote that the Olympics would be a battle between athletes and artists. But Coach Ness said that wasn't fair. Kristi's free skating routine was very difficult technically. It just didn't have a triple Axel.

"Kristi doesn't lift weights twice a week to be called fluff," Ness said. The coach believed her student was the perfect combination of athlete and artist.

As it turned out, that's what the judges thought, too.

Still, mistakes by Tonya and Midori helped put Kristi in position to win the gold.

Ito seemed to get more nervous during the practice days leading up to the competition. It showed during the short program. Ito fell on the required jump combination, and that left her fourth after the first round.

Harding fell doing her triple Axel and finished sixth. Later, she said she was suffering from jet lag and had made a mistake in flying to France three days before the competition.

Kristi and Nancy Kerrigan both skated clean short programs. They finished 1-2. If Kristi managed to finish first or second in the free skating, she would win the gold.

Coach Ness was asked if she would play it safe and take out Kristi's hardest moves. No way, she said.

The top six skaters were in the last group of competitors, and Kristi led off. She started off very strongly, hitting her triples and spins and skating her routine with great artistry. But halfway through, she fell on a relatively easy jump, the triple loop. That shook her up a bit, and she doubled a planned triple Salchow.

The judges gave her five 5.7s and four 5.8s for technical merit. She got eight 5.9s and one 5.8 for artistic impression. The judges left room for someone to beat Kristi, but that person would have to be perfect.

Nobody was. Not Ito. Not Harding. Not Kerrigan. Not Bonaly. Not Chen Lu of China. Everyone of them fell. There were other mistakes, too.

Kristi was the champion—the first American to win the gold medal since her heroine, Dorothy Hamill. Kristi was so stunned, Nancy Kerrigan had to push her out onto the ice for the awards ceremony,

But it was no fluke. Kristi went on to worlds and won there, too. Soon after, she turned professional, where she continues to be a top competitor.

OKSANA BAIUL

In 1991, the International Skating Union made a rules change that would enable young talented skaters like Oksana Baiul and Michelle Kwan to move to the top of the sport faster.

Without it, Oksana might never have made the 1994 Olympics, let alone have won them at age 16. Michelle probably would not have made the U.S. world team at 13.

Of course, getting kids to the top of a sport traditionally dominated by young men and women was not the reason the ISU voted to eliminate compulsory figures from international competition. But that was a side effect.

The rule change was made because skaters, fans, and TV networks preferred free skating to the old-fashioned tracing of fancy figure 8s. Though the figures are the roots out

Oksana Baiul was just 16 years old when she won the gold at the 1994 Olympics. She wore a bandage on her leg to cover the stitches she needed after colliding with another skater the day before her long program.

of which modern figure skating grew, they seemed to have little meaning in the late 1980s and 1990s.

They were boring to skate and boring to watch. Television wouldn't show the figures portion of competition on the air.

Learning the figures also was expensive, because they took years of lessons and "patch," or practice, time to learn. Skaters perfected their Axel and Lutz jumps long before they mastered their "left rocker curve."

Once the figures that had slowed their progress were gone, young athletic skaters with great jumping ability were able to rise quickly through the ranks.

In terms of the skating world, Oksana Baiul literally came out of nowhere in 1993 to become the youngest world figure skating champion since Sonja Henie in 1936. The favorites that year were veteran competitors Nancy Kerrigan and Tonya Harding of the United States and Surya Bonaly of France.

The 1993 worlds were only Oksana's fourth international competition. It was a miracle that she ever got to that competition at all.

A native of Dnepropetrovsk, Ukraine, in the old Soviet Union, Oksana was 13 when her mother died of cancer. For all intents and purposes, she was an orphan; Oksana had not seen her father since she was a baby. Her mother's parents also were dead.

Oksana lived for a while with her coach, Stanislav Korytek, but times were bad for him, too. The Soviet government had collapsed, and its 15 former republics had become separate countries. The economy was terrible. When Korytek was offered a job in Canada, he felt he had to take it. He left Oksana behind.

Before he left, though, Korytek asked another famous Soviet coach to instruct his talented young skater. Galina Zmievskaya, coach of 1992 Olympic skating champion Viktor Petrenko, did that and more. She made Oksana part of her family.

Coach Galina took Oksana away from Dnepropetrovsk to her home in Odessa. Oksana moved into a bedroom with Galina's younger daughter, Galya. Viktor, who married Galina's older daughter, Nina, bought Oksana new blades and boots. He also gave her fabric from his costumes for skating dresses.

Oksana still missed her mother and grandparents, but her skating and her new family helped her to laugh again. Her emotion showed through her skating and made audiences love her. Judges admired her beautiful skating and spins. And she could jump well, too.

She won the 1993 Ukrainian nationals soon after she moved to Odessa and qualified for the 1993 Europeans. They would be just her third competition outside of the old Soviet Union and her first major international event.

The lack of experience didn't bother Oksana at all. She finished second to France's Surya Bonaly. Then she went on to the worlds, where she skated even better.

Oksana finished second to Nancy Kerrigan in the short program. Then, when Nancy fell apart and skated poorly in the free skating, Oksana won the long program over Surya. Oksana was the new world champion at age 15!

Figure skating experts didn't know what to think of Oksana. Was her world victory a happy accident? Was she a fast-rising star who would burn out just as quickly? Or was she just starting a long reign as the world's skating queen?

The answer came a year later, when Oksana defeated Nancy again at the 1994 Olympics.

The world had been expecting a duel between Nancy and her chief American rival, Tonya Harding. A man had attacked Nancy at the U.S. nationals and hurt her knee. She had to drop out of the competition, and Tonya won. Later, police linked the crime to Tonya's husband. They believed he tried to have Nancy hurt so it would be easier for Tonya to win the nationals and the Olympics. Tonya was also linked to the attack and had to sue for the right to go to the Olympics.

Tonya might as well have stayed home. She skated poorly in Hamar, Norway. She was never in the chase for the gold medal.

Nancy Kerrigan also skated beautifully and won the silver at the 1994 Olympics. Her leg too was injured—in an attack several months before by an associate of rival Tonya Harding's husband.

Instead, Oksana and Nancy staged one of the closest and most dramatic duels in Olympic skating history.

Nancy won the short program, seven judges to two. The next day, during a practice session for the upcoming free skating, Oksana collided on the ice with another skater and cut her leg and hurt her back.

Though she was stiff and sore, Oksana took a couple of shots for pain and went out to compete the night after the accident. Neither skater was perfect, but both were very good.

The judges had tough decisions to make. Oksana ended up winning the long program and the gold medal, by a margin of five judges to four. The deciding judge scored Oksana just a tenth of a point higher than Nancy.

After the Olympics, Oksana moved to the United States with Coach Galina and her family. Oksana and Nancy both turned professional, and nowadays they sometimes compete against one another for cash prizes.

Because Oksana was so young when she turned pro, some people thought she might ask for her amateur status back so she could qualify for the 1998 Olympics. But Oksana decided she liked life as a pro. She enjoys skating for her fans without the pressure of competition. Somebody else will have to succeed her as Olympic champion.

In March 1996, Michelle Kwan of Torrance, California, won her first world title. Just 15, she was the third youngest world titlist behind Sonja Henie and Oksana. Other good young skaters in the United States included 1995 U.S. champion Nicole Bobek of Chicago, Sydne Vogel of Anchorage, Alaska; Tara Lipinski of Sugarland, Texas; and Shelby Lyons of Oswego, New York.

But Michelle had the longest list of credentials. Michelle already had spent two years as a "lady in waiting" when she won her first U.S. and world crowns.

The world got its first look at Michelle at the 1994 U.S. Nationals where Nancy Kerrigan

Michelle Kwan was already a major presence on the international circuit at age 12. She won a world championship at age 15.

was attacked. Michelle was 13 and skating in only her second senior nationals.

After Nancy was forced to drop out of the competition, Tonya Harding won the title. But tiny Michelle—she was 4' 9" and weighed 77 pounds—finished a surprising second. U.S. skating officials named Nancy and Tonya to the Olympic team, but Michelle was the first alternate.

She flew to Norway, too, though she didn't get to stay in the Olympic Village. But she stayed in shape just in case Tonya was barred from competing. Tonya got to skate for the Olympics, but she was disqualified from the U.S. team before the worlds. Michelle took her place and finished eighth.

She looked so young and tiny among the older skaters. Still, everyone began predicting she be would the sport's new amateur star.

In 1995, she had gone to the U.S. nationals with the heavy burden of being the favorite at the age of 14. Though she had all the jumps and spins and steps, she was still very young. In contrast, Nancy Kerrigan was 23 when she won her first crown in 1993.

If the ISU hadn't eliminated compulsory figures, Michelle might still have been in novice or juniors working to perfect them.

Michelle's coach, Frank Carroll, thought his student was ready for the challenge, though. He told reporters that Michelle had matured and become a more artistic skater.

Then Michelle made a mistake in her short program, bobbling her required jump combination. The judges scored her third behind veteran Tonia Kwiatkowski and Nicole Bobek, 16. Nicole is an extremely talented and beautiful skater who has usually ran out of gas in the long program. She has also been criticized for not working as hard as skaters like Kwan.

But not this time. Bobek had a new coach, Richard Callaghan, who was strict with her. In 1995 she was fit enough to get through the program without getting tired. She didn't make the kind of mistakes tired skaters usually make. She skated a beautiful program and got good scores. But there still was room for Michelle to win.

Michelle skated last and she skated well, too—until the final jump. Michelle fell on a triple Lutz. Nicole won the U.S. title, eight judges to one.

Maybe Michelle *was* too young.

The judges at the 1995 worlds in Birmingham, England, seemed to think so. She skated the most difficult short and long programs at the competition—and she did so while skating almost flawlessly. Her long program was so good that the audience gave her a long standing ovation.

But the judges placed her fourth. Chen Lu of China was champion, Surya Bonaly was second, and Nicole was third.

The only thing those three skaters had that Michelle didn't was maturity. They looked grown up. Michelle looked like a little girl.

That changed over the next year, though. Coach Frank Carroll gave Michelle a different look. Instead of wearing her hair in a pony tail, she wore it in a braided bun. Frank persuaded

Nicole Bobek is one of America's bright hopes for the future.

her parents to let her wear eye makeup when she skated.

Michelle worked very hard all year. She improved her artistry—her facial expressions and her arm movements. And she became extremely consistent. She competed in three international events—and won all three.

Then she went to the nationals in San Jose, California, and made her unbeaten streak four in a row. Nicole, meanwhile, had changed coaches again. She had been injured, and she aggravated the ankle injury in the short program and again warming up for the long program. She had to drop out of the competition.

At the world championships in Edmonton, Canada, Michele narrowly defeated defending champion Chen Lu in the short program.

Lu was not about to give up her title easily. She skated before Michelle in the long program, and she was wonderful. Her program was very difficult. It incorporated six triple jumps, including two in combination. And she landed all of them without mistakes. Two judges gave her perfect 6.0s.

Michelle couldn't help but hear the scores Lu got. But Coach Frank told her there still was room for her to win. She'd just have to do her best.

"I got myself down to earth and said, 'Just go for it. Go for everything. Why not?" Michelle said later.

And so she did. Michelle also landed six triple jumps, two in combination. Then, as she neared the end of the program, she added a seventh. It was perfect, too! She had one more jump than Lu. That would make the difference.

Michelle won the long program, six judges to three. She became the third youngest world champion in history, behind Sonja Henie and Oksana Baiul.

The challenge that faced Michelle after the 1996 worlds was to stay on top for two years, until the 1998 Winter Olympics. As is true for all athletes, Michelle Kwan is finding out that it is easier to get to the top than it is to stay there.

Among Michelle's competition is the most recent in the line of figure skating stars to make it to the top—the youngest women's national champion in history, Tara Lipinski. At the age of 14, Lipinski executed seven clean triple jumps in her free skate program, as well as something never seen before in a women's U.S. championship—a triple loop–triple loop combination.

Tara's win gave her the opportunity to represent the United States at the 1997 World Championships held in Switzerland. Again, she was unbeatable and broke yet another age barrier. She became the youngest female skater to ever hold the title of World Champion.

For someone so young, Tara has a very long list of achievements. Prior to joining the ranks of the senior skaters, Tara medaled at both the national novice and junior levels. In 1995 she became the youngest gold medalist in the history of the U.S. Olympic Festival, an annual event where the most promising newcomers in many sports compete.

With her passion for skating and her determination to succeed, Tara Lipinski is perhaps the United States' brightest hope for the 1998 Winter Olympics and another women's figure skating gold medal.

CHRONOLOGY

1924   Sonja Henie of Norway skates in her first Olympics at age 11 and finishes last.

1928   Sonja Henie, 15 years old, wins the first of three Olympic gold medals.

1936   Sonja Henie wins her third and last Olympic title.

1956   Tenley Albright becomes the first American woman to win an Olympic figure skating championship.

1960   American Carol Heiss succeeds Albright as the Olympic figure skating champion.

1964   Peggy Fleming wins the first of five straight U.S. championships.

1968   Peggy Fleming becomes the United States' third Olympic women's figure skating champion.

1976   Dorothy Hamill becomes the fourth American woman to win an Olympic figure skating championship.

1984   Katarina Witt wins the first of her two Olympic and four world figure skating championships.

1988   Katarina Witt becomes first female back-to-back winner of Olympic figure skating titles since Sonja Henie.

1992   Kristi Yamaguchi becomes the fifth American woman to win an Olympic figure skating championship.

1994   Oksana Baiul of the Ukraine, at age 16, narrowly defeats Nancy Kerrigan for the Olympic figure-skating championship.

1996   American Michelle Kwan becomes the third-youngest women's world figure-skating champion (after Henie and Baiul).

1997   Texas-born Tara Lipinski becomes both the youngest National Champion and World Champion at the age of 14.

SUGGESTIONS FOR FURTHER READING

Brennan, Christine. *Inside Edge*. New York: Scribner, 1996.

Coffey, Wayne, and Filip Bondy. *Dreams of Gold: The Nancy Kerrigan Story*. New York: St. Martin's Press, 1994.

Hollander, Phyllis and Zander, eds. 1984 Sarajevo, Yugoslavia: *The Complete Handbook of the Olympic Winter Games*. New York: Signet Books, 1983.

McMane, Fred, and Cathrine Wolf. *Winning Women*. New York: Bantam Books, 1996.

Morse, Charles and Ann. *Peggy Fleming*. Mankato, MN: Creative Education, 1974.

Sheffield, Robert and Richard Woodward, *The Ice Skating Book*. New York: Universe Books, 1980.

Trenary, Jill, with Dale Mitch. *The Day I Skated for the Gold*. New York: Simon and Schuster, 1989.

Van Steenwyk, Elizabeth. *Peggy Fleming: Cameo of a Champion*. New York: McGraw-Hill, 1978.

Wallechinsky, David. *The Complete Book of the Olympics*. New York: Viking Press, 1984.

PICTURE CREDITS

INDEX

ABOUT THE AUTHOR

POHLA SMITH has been a journalist for nearly 25 years. She was a writer and columnist for *United Press International* from 1973-1991, specializing in figure skating, gymnastics, and horse racing over her last decade with the wire service. Recently Ms. Smith has been teaching at the University of Pittsburgh and acting as writing coach/assistant metro editor for *The North Hills News Record*, a Gannett Newspaper. Ms. Smith's work frequently is seen in *Sports Illustrated for Kids* and *USA Today*. She is the author of *Head-to-Head Basketball: Shaquille O'Neal and Hakeem Olajuwon*.